Learn About the Nile Crocodile

By Tiana Price

© 2019 Tiana Price

COVER IMAGE

https://www.flickr.com/photos/rod_waddington/15024048528/

ADDITIONAL IMAGES

https://www.flickr.com/photos/nickwebb/2902531040/

https://www.flickr.com/photos/andymorffew/44335259425/

https://www.flickr.com/photos/pamas/20040001103/

https://www.flickr.com/photos/davidstanleytravel/11510492003/

https://www.flickr.com/photos/phaselockedloop/32301947742/

https://www.flickr.com/photos/47847725@N04/4530698197/

https://www.flickr.com/photos/wildlife_encounters/13869043013/

https://www.flickr.com/photos/pamas/20025021606/

https://www.flickr.com/photos/hisgett/3308761119/

https://www.flickr.com/photos/shankaronline/8455426960/

Contents

INTRODUCTION

Nile crocodiles are very large reptiles. They are native to Africa and are found throughout the Sub-Saharan area. They live mostly in freshwater.

They are carnivorous and eat only meat. They are very aggressive and will eat almost anything. They are also very social crocodiles. They like to lay in the sun with their mouths open. Males and females can be identified by how they look. They are very long-lived animals and have very few enemies.

CHARACTERISTICS

Nile crocodiles spend most of their time in the water or very close to water. They use water to hide in order to surprise and attack food. They are often seen lying in the sun on river banks with their mouths open. Laying in the sun helps them regulate their body temperature.

They have very thick bronze colored skin. They have long powerful tails that they use to swim as fast as 20 miles per hour when they are in water. They have very short legs compared to the length of their body, but they can still run over eight miles an hour!

They have very powerful jaws lined with cone-shaped teeth. Their jaws are some of the strongest in the world and this helps them to capture food. Nile crocodiles can only stay under water for a few minutes, but can swim long distances if the need arises. If they do not move, they can stay under water for two hours. When they bask in the sun, birds will come to clean their teeth and pick leeches from their mouths.

Nile crocodiles are very caring parents. They female will stay close and guard the nest when they have babies. They also care for the babies and protect them from enemies.

APPEARANCE

Nile crocodiles are long reptiles. They also have darker lines going across their backs that helps them camouflage themselves in shallow water. They tuck their short legs close to their body so they can swim fast. They have long tails that are higher than they are wide.

LIFE STAGES

Nile crocodiles have three life stages. The first life stage is the egg stage. This stage begins when the female lays eggs (between 25 and 80) one to two months after mating. She lays her eggs in a nest dug 20 inches deep in sandy river banks. Their nests are then covered and the eggs hatch around 90 days.

After the eggs hatch, the juvenile life stage begins. This is the second life stage. After they are born until they are two years old, the female crocodile will guard her juveniles very closely. Although they are guarded by their mother, the juveniles will hunt and feed themselves.

When they are older than two years, they are on their own. They will live in groups with other crocodiles, but they do not reach the adult life stage until they are 12 to 16 years old. The adult life stage is the final life stage.

LIFE SPAN

Nile crocodiles are very long lived reptiles. They can live longer in the wild than in captivity. In the wild they will live 70 to 100 years, but in captivity (like zoos) they do not usually live longer than 60 years.

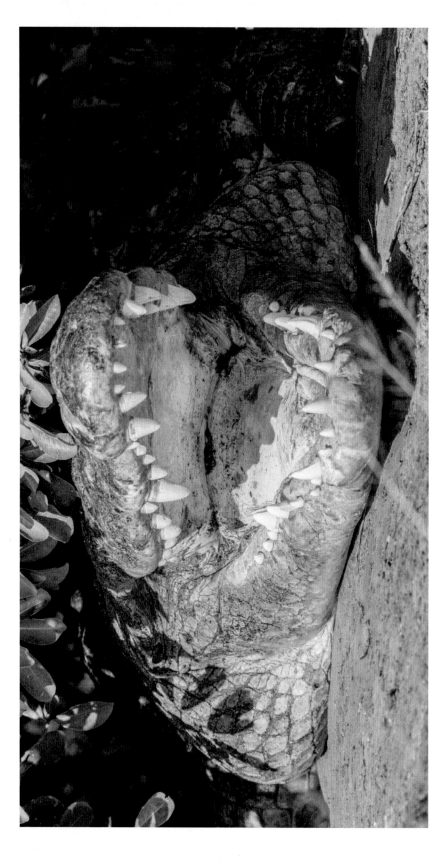

SIZE

Nile crocodiles are the second largest crocodiles in the world and are the largest crocodiles in Africa. They are 11 to 12 inches long when they are born, but grow quickly. Males are larger than females with males being 30% larger on average. Only saltwater crocodiles that live in Florida and Australia are larger.

Adult females grow to be 7 to 12 feet in length and weigh 88 to 550 pounds. Adult males care generally 10 to 16 feet in length and weigh 330 to 1,540 pounds. There have been some extremely large crocodiles found and recorded to weigh as much as 2400 pounds!

HABITAT

Nile crocodiles are native to Sub-Saharan Africa. They live mainly in freshwater habitat along rivers, but they can be found in some saltwater lagoons and deltas. They need areas with sandy soil and plenty of open sunny areas where they can bask to regulate their body temperature. They do not have a specialized diet so that does not restrict their range.

They have been introduced into some areas that they are not native. They have been found in the wild in Florida. They are known to be able to adapt to most areas where they find and abundance of animals to eat, water, and places where they can rest in the sun.

DIET

Nile crocodiles eat only meat. They have been known to eat fish, reptiles, other crocodiles, snakes, deer, wildebeest, birds, and even people. They will even eat large snakes like pythons. These crocodiles will try to eat anything that ends up in their mouths. This is what makes it easy for them to survive in places that are not their native habitat when they are introduced to new areas.

FRIENDS AND ENEMIES

Nile crocodiles are very social with each other. They are found in large groups and can communicate with each other through sounds they make. However, they also fight with each other to establish dominance. Female crocodiles will protect their juveniles and they communicate with each other through calls as well. Some birds are also friends with crocodiles.

They are very large and considered the top predator where they live. This means that they do not have very many enemies. Birds, reptiles, and some mammals will attack the juveniles. But when this happens, the juveniles will call out and their mother will come to protect them. People are also enemies of crocodiles. People have been known to attack crocodiles for food.

SUITABILITY AS PETS

Nile crocodiles are not suitable as pets. They are very large animals and need a lot of space. They need to eat a lot of food and can become aggressive with all other animals and people. Crocodiles should not be kept as pets.

COLOR ME

COLOR ME

COLOR ME

COLOR ME

COLOR ME

COLOR ME

More Picture Books by Tiana Price

Learn About the Vervet Monkey, Vol 6

https://www.amazon.com/dp/1707251800

Learn About the Three Toed Sloth, Vol 29

https://www.amazon.com/dp/1670461327

Learn About the Tasmanian Tiger, Vol 28

https://www.amazon.com/dp/1670440834

Learn About the Canada Lynx, Vol 14

https://www.amazon.com/dp/170808908X

Learn About the Galapagos Penguin, Vol 35

https://www.amazon.com/dp/1674121245

Made in the USA
Monee, IL
20 April 2022